First
Facts®

ELITE MILITARY FORCES

THE NAVY SEALs

by Jennifer M. Besel

CAPSTONE PRESS
a capstone imprint

First Facts is published by Capstone Press,
1710 Roe Crest Drive, North Mankato, Minnesota 56003.
www.capstonepub.com

 Books published by Capstone Press are manufactured with paper
containing at least 10 percent post-consumer waste.

Library of Congress Cataloging-in-Publication Data
Besel, Jennifer M.
  The Navy SEALs / by Jennifer M. Besel.
     p. cm.—(First facts. Elite military forces)
  Includes bibliographical references and index.
  Summary: "Provides information on the U.S. Navy SEALs, including their training,
missions, and equipment"—Provided by publisher.
  ISBN 978-1-4296-5380-0 (library binding)
  1. United States. Navy. SEALs—Juvenile literature. I. Title. II. Series.
  VG87.B39 2011
  359.9'84—dc22   2010029387

Editorial credits:
Christine Peterson, editor; Matt Bruning, designer; Laura Manthe, production specialist

Photo credits
Alamy/Ilian Gun, 17(pistol); Shutterstock/koh sze kiat, cover; RCPPHOTO, 17(rifle);
U.S. Marine Corps photo by Lance Cpl. Megan E. Sindelar, 5; U.S. Navy photo by MC2
Kyle D. Gahlau, 13, 14;; MC3 Robyn Gerstenslager, 21; PHC Andrew Mckaskle, 9, 19;
PH2 Eric S. Logsdon, 11; PH2; Marjorie McNamee, 6

Artistic Effects
iStockphoto/Brett Charlton, Craig DeBourbon; Shutterstock/koh sze kiat, Maksym
Bondarchuk, Masonjar, Péter Gudella, reventon2527, Serg64, Tom Grundy

**Capstone Press thanks the U.S. Special Operations Command, MacDill AFB in
Tampa, Florida, for its assistance with this book**

Printed in the United States of America in North Mankato, Minnesota.
032012   006647R

TABLE OF CONTENTS

An airplane soars over the ocean. Inside, U.S. Navy SEALs prepare for the mission. Below the airplane, pirates are holding a U.S. ship captain **hostage** in a lifeboat. A Navy **destroyer** waits in the waves nearby. But there's nothing it can do to help.

hostage: a person held prisoner by an enemy

destroyer: a warship

Suddenly, the SEALs parachute from the airplane. They land in the water. Climbing aboard the destroyer, the SEALs aim their rifles at the lifeboat.

The pirates draw their weapons. The SEALs know the captain's life is in danger. They fire, and the pirates go down. Quickly, SEALs slide down ropes to the lifeboat. They rescue the hostage and bring him to safety.

U.S. Navy SEALs are some of the best trained military men in the world. SEAL missions take place in the sea, from the air, and on land. In fact, that's what SEAL stands for.

SEALs work underwater without being noticed. They set bombs in rivers to destroy an enemy's bridges. They swim underwater to get into enemy territory. They are trained and ready to defend the United States.

SEALs also work in the air and on land. SEALs parachute into enemy territory. Once on land, they spy on enemy **troops**. SEALs are trained to stop **terrorists**.

troops: soldiers who are part of a group

terrorist: someone who uses violence to achieve a goal

FACT

Current U.S. rules allow only men to be selected for Navy SEALs.

BECOMING A NAVY SEAL

Navy SEAL training is among the hardest in the military. Sailors go through more than 30 months of classes and physical training. Those who pass become SEALs.

The first level of training is Basic Underwater Demolition/SEAL (BUD/S). During BUD/S sailors do hundreds of push-ups a day. They run miles on sandy beaches. Teams race carrying heavy logs.

FACT

The fourth week of BUD/S is one of the worst. The men get less than five hours of sleep during the entire week of training.

FACT

Only one in five men will finish BUD/S training.

During training, sailors spend most of their time in the water. They learn to control small boats in the ocean. They train to use **scuba** gear.

Sailors also learn how to keep from drowning. Trainers tie up the men's hands and feet. The men then have to swim and bounce up for air.

scuba: equipment used to breathe underwater

A SEAL's EQUIPMENT

On missions, SEALs bring weapons to get the job done. Each man usually carries a CAR-15 rifle. For battles, they might use rocket and grenade launchers. The smaller 9mm pistol is often one of their weapons too.

9mm pistol

CAR-15 rifle

On secret missions, SEALs use the SEAL Delivery Vehicle (SDV). These boats take off from a submarine. They travel completely underwater.

To reach enemy beaches, SEALs use a Rigid **Hull** Inflatable Boat (RHIB). This sturdy boat can handle rough waters. It travels 40 miles (64 kilometers) per hour.

hull: the main body of a boat

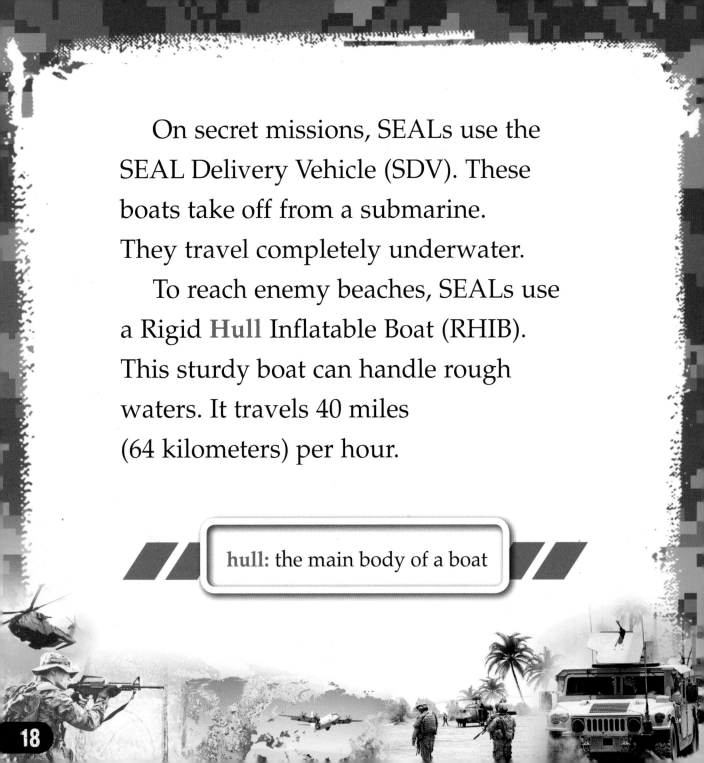

SDV

JUMPING IN

Navy SEALs are always prepared to fight for the United States. They rescue hostages. SEALs slip into enemy lands to gather information. By sea, air, or land, SEALs are ready to jump in and complete the mission.

FACT

During missions in Afghanistan, SEALs have destroyed more than 500,000 pounds (226,800 kilograms) of enemy weapons.

GLOSSARY

destroyer (di-STROI-ur)—a small, fast warship that uses guns, missiles, and torpedoes to protect other ships from submarines

hostage (HOSS-tij)—a person held prisoner by an enemy

hull (HUL)—the main body or casing of a boat, ship, tank, or armored vehicle

scuba (SKOO-buh)—self-contained underwater breathing apparatus; divers use scuba equipment to breathe underwater

terrorist (TER-ur-ist)—someone who uses violence to achieve a goal

troops (TROOPS)—soldiers who are part of a group

READ MORE

David, Jack. *Navy SEALs*. Armed Forces. Minneapolis: Bellwether Media, 2009.

Jackson, Kay. *Navy Submarines in Action*. Amazing Military Vehicles. New York: PowerKids Press, 2009.

Yomtov, Nelson. *Navy SEALs in Action*. Special Ops. New York: Bearport Pub., 2008.

INTERNET SITES

FactHound offers a safe, fun way to find Internet sites related to this book. All of the sites on FactHound have been researched by our staff.

Here's all you do:

Visit *www.facthound.com*

Type in this code: 9781429653800

Super-cool stuff!

Check out projects, games and lots more at
www.capstonekids.com

INDEX